Don the Beachcomber's

Little
Hawaiian
Tropical Drink
Cookbook

Don the Beachcomber's

Little Hawaiian Tropical Drink Cookbook

Arnold Bitner and Phoebe Beach

Mutual Publishing

Copyright © 2004 by Mutual Publishing

Adapted from *Hawai'i Tropical Rum Drinks &
Cuisine by Don the Beachcomber*

ISBN-10: 1-56647-692-5
ISBN-13: 978-1-56647-692-8

Library of Congress Catalog Card Number:
2004112028

Design by Emily R. Lee
All photography by Douglas Peebles

First Printing October 2004
Second Printing , October 2005
Third Printing October 2007
Fourth Printing, October 2010

Mutual Publishing, LLC
1215 Center Street, Suite 210
Honolulu, Hawai'i 96816
Ph: 808-732-1709 / Fax: 808-734-4094
email: info@mutualpublishing.com
www.mutualpublishing.com

Printed in Korea

Table of Contents

Introduction

Selling a Dream

A sparkling horizon punctuated by palm trees, languid afternoons on a sandy beach—these are the things that vacationers the world over dream of when they think of Hawai'i. And what do those vacationers drink in their dreams? Why, colorful drinks decorated with orchids and tiny paper parasols, of course, drinks served by pretty *pareu*-clad girls in bars festooned with pandanus mats, seashells, exotic flowers and a few tikis here and there.

Hawai'i as tropical paradise—it's an inescapable image. And yet it didn't grow solely out of the Islands' natural beauty and culture. It also grew from the dreams of a few creative individuals. Key of those was Donn Beach, a.k.a. Don the Beachcomber, a man who almost single-handedly transformed Hawai'i's culinary and hospitality scene—a man who all but invented tropical drinks and the exotic themed restaurant.

Don the Beachcomber gazing out over Waikīkī beach in the early 1950s.

The Making of a Restaurateur

Donn Beach was a native of Louisiana, but he had a restless spirit that by the time he was twenty-four had taken him to Jamaica, Australia, Papua New Guinea, the Marquesas, Tahiti, and, finally, Hollywood. He arrived in Hollywood in 1931, at the start of the Great Depression and during the depths of Prohibition. He scrambled to make ends meet, and often ate in the soup kitchens of Chinatown (where he mastered Chinese cooking). He found odd jobs whenever he could: parking cars, running rum, and bootlegging whiskey.

With a little money in his pocket, Donn began to eat his dinners at Simon's Cafeteria, where a meal cost twenty-five cents. Here, he made

Don the Beachcomber resting inside his original Don the Beachcomber restaurant in Los Angeles, 1934.

friends with David Niven, Marlene Dietrich and Tubby Broccoli. Soon, he became a technical advisor on several South Seas movies, including *Moon of Manakura* and *Hell's Half Acre*. Money may have been in short supply, but Don the Beachcomber always had his dreams and his South Seas expertise—not to mention spears, shells, and any manner of other props.

By the end of 1933, Donn thought he had more than a clue about how the bar and restaurant business should be operated. On a little street off Hollywood Boulevard he discovered a "For Rent" sign on a tailor shop that had gone belly up. He got a five-year lease at thirty dollars a month on the strength of his word and a handshake. The space was thirteen by thirty feet. He set

Don the Beachcomber with Oswald Henriques in Jamaica.

up a bar with stools that accommodated thirty people and five small tables with chairs. Then he decorated the place with his South Seas artifacts, some old nets and parts of ships he'd found along the San Pedro waterfront. A handcrafted driftwood sign spelling out "Don's Beachcomber" was hung out front. Two young Filipino men served the tables and two more assisted behind the bar.

Donn's timing was perfect. By 1934, Prohibition had been repealed and, recognizing that people hadn't had a decent drink during the previous "fourteen years of darkness," the new bar keeper started concocting some of his most famous exotic rum drinks. The first was the Sumatra Kula, which sold for twenty-five cents. Others with tropical-sounding names soon followed, all made with thirty-year-old rum: the fourteen-ounce Zombie (which sold for $1.75 and contained five different rums), Mai Tai Swizzle, Beachcomber's Gold, Missionary's Downfall, Cuban Daiquiri, Pearl Diver, and Don's Pearl. A genuine

Don the Beachcomber behind the bar of his original Don the Beachcomber restaurant in L.A., 1934.

pearl was placed into every fifth Don's Pearl.

By the time Don the Beachcomber arrived in Honolulu in 1946, his Polynesian-themed restaurant/nightclubs were well established. His formula for creating an exotic setting out of rattan furniture from the Philippines, tropical rum drinks, and Chinese dishes worked very well in Hawai'i. Donn hired top entertainment: Some of the more famous names who performed at the Beachcomber were Alfred Apaka, Rosalei Stevens, Haunani Kahalewai, and Iolani Luahine. Donn also brought in entertainers from Tahiti and Fiji, many of whom went on to enjoy fame in their own right. Donn's greatest fame, of course, has remained the tropical drink. In all, he concocted more than ninety original Don the Beachcomber rum drinks, many of which are still well-known and popular the world over. You'll find those recipes here. So kick back, don an aloha shirt, and start mixing as you envision palm trees and sandy beaches—the dream is alive and well.

Rum The NECTAR of the Gods

Throughout the world, and for more than four hundred years, rum has been recognized as a drink to quench the thirst, heal the sick, and imbue strong men with the will to do bold deeds. The potency of rum has been immortalized in song and story—where rum has flowed, action has followed. It was in the bellies of pirates Captain Kidd, Sir Henry Morgan, and Blackbeard; with the heroes of the American Revolution, including George Washington; with the soldiers and sailors of both land and sea forces of America and England.

The drink itself is a distillate made from pure cane sugar. Rum's flavor and quality are determined by the climate and the soil in which the sugar cane is grown, by the method of fermentation, and by the age of the spirit itself. Don the Beachcomber dedicated much of his life to learning the secrets and customs of rum and rum drinking, and included in this book are forty-one original rum drinks he created. As you will discover, with the guide of Don the Beachcomber's practiced hand and discriminating judgment, rum truly became the "Nectar of the Gods."

By 1945, Don the Beachcomber was the largest single user of the rum in the entire world. He served more than 325,000 cases of the stuff each year. Drink menus in his restaurants listed sixty of his original rum concoctions; rum menus listed a whopping 138 brands of rum, which came from sixteen different countries.

Donn's dedication to providing the best rums for his restaurants led him to travel extensively. He became a student of rums in the islands of the West Indies and spent years searching the islands of Cuba, Puerto Rico, Jamaica, Haiti, Trinidad, and Barbados for the finest available. He developed close friendships with Oswald Henriques of J. Wray & Nephew Ltd., and Fred Myers, owner of Myers's in Jamaica. On his trips, Donn would try rum after rum, as well as various combinations of rums. Over time, he developed an extensive knowledge of the rum distilling process and a keen sense for flavor nuances. Several rums were specially blended under his direction so that they would be suitable to mix with various tropical fruits.

The recipes that follow are the result of Donn Beach's many years of rum connoisseurship. Many of the rums available to Don the Beachcomber from the 1930s to the 1950s are no longer manufactured, so we have included recommendations for replacement rums where necessary. Look for the notation "*Recommended rum substitutions" on the recipes included here.

Original Rum Drinks

Honey Cream Mix

One part sweet butter
One part honey

Heat the honey and butter separately.
Do not boil. When sufficiently heated,
pour honey over the sweet butter
into one container. Turn off the heat.
Commence whipping with a wire
whip until both ingredients are well
blended. Store in freezer until
ready to use.

The Greatest of All Drinks

Don the Beachcomber always claimed: "Rum holds certain therapeutic values and is the purest spirit made, the greatest of all drinks because it is distilled from sugar cane, and is easily assimilated into the body's system."

Planter's
Rum Punch

3/4 ounce fresh lime juice
3/4 ounce Honey Cream Mix
1-1/2 ounces fresh pineapple juice
1-1/2 ounces Jamaica Dagger Punch
    dark rum*
1-1/2 ounces soda water
1 dash Angostura bitters

Pour all of the above into a blender.
Add eight (8) ounces cracked ice. Shake
for 1/2 minute and pour contents into
an appropriate glass. Serve with a straw.
Add a finger of fresh pineapple and
cherry on sticks or skewers.

Recommended rum substitution:
        1-1/2 ounces Appleton Estate rum

Beachcomber's Gold

This delectable, mellow cocktail with its old rums, Tahitian limes, and wild honey was Marlene Dietrich's favorite. Wake up your taste buds with this tasty before-dinner potion.

1/3 ounce lime juice
3/4 ounce passion fruit juice
1/2 ounce honey
1 ounce Puerto Rican light rum*
1/2 ounce Jamaica light rum*
2 dashes Angostura bitters

Pour into blender. Add six (6) ounces cracked ice. Blend for 15 seconds. Strain into a frozen glass with ice molded into the shape of a fan.

Recommended rum substitutions:
1 ounce Bacardi light rum
1/2 ounce Myers's platinum rum

BEACHcomber's
Daiquiri

2 ounces Cuban white rum
Juice of one large lime
1 ounce Cointreau

Place a handful of
dime-size cracked ice into a
blender and shake for 15 to 20
seconds. Serve in large six (6) ounce
champagne bowl glass with ice igloo.

The Inventor

After opening his famous Don the Beachcomber restaurant in Hollywood in 1933, Donn Beach became the serious inventor of more than ninety exotic tropical rum concoctions, including the Mai Tai, originally called the Mai Tai Swizzle; the Zombie; Missionary's Downfall and the Beachcomber's Daiquiri, each drink created for a mood, climate or time of day. As an example, the Zombie and the Test Pilot were created for afternoon sipping, while the Beachcomber's Gold and Beachcomber's Daiquiri were for early evening around sundown. The Mai Tai and the Pi Yi were for later.

Beachcomber's
Rum Barrel

3/4 ounce lime juice
1/2 ounce honey
1/4 ounce Fassionola*
1 ounce orange juice
1 ounce pineapple juice
1 ounce grapefruit juice
1 ounce soda
2 ounces Ron Rican light rum**
2 ounces Myers's rum**
1 dash each Angostura bitters,
        Pernod, grenadine, foam

Blend with eight(8)
ounces cracked ice.
Pour into a tall glass.

* Fassionola - Fruit flavored blends used mainly by bars.
Use fruit punch as a substitution.

** Recommended rum substitution:

2 ounces Myers's Original dark rum

Ambassador of Rum

Over the years the Beachcomber searched the Caribbean and West Indies for the finest rums available. On visits to Jamaica and Cuba spanning a number of years, he spent many days walking the sugar cane fields and studying the processing procedures at the distilling plants. In 1939 in Jamaica, his title of Ambassador of Rum was officially bestowed on him by leaders of the rum industry.

Don the Beachcomber's Plantation Punch

1-1/2 ounces Puerto Rican light rum*
1 ounce Jamaica rum*
1 ounce Demarara rum*
1/4 ounce Falernum
1/2 ounce Triple Sec
1 ounce fresh lime juice
2 ounces club soda

Twist lime peel into shaker to obtain oil. Shake well with ice. Serve in a Zombie glass. Decorate with a spear of fresh pineapple and several sprigs of mint. Locate a nice, cool, comfortable spot under a palm, sip drink slowly and let the world go by.

* Recommended rum substitutions:

1-1/2 ounces Bacardi light rum
1 ounce Myers's platinum rum
1 ounce Lemon Hart (80 proof)

The Plantation

Donn's "Plantation" in Encino, California, was a re-creation of a South Seas paradise, completely furnished with curios he had been collecting over the years. Here, among the pandanus-covered huts and lily-filled pools, were Gala and Pagos, the Beachcomber's three-hundred-pound Galapagos Turtles. They lived at the "Plantation" and provided constant entertainment at the private lūʻau held for his many friends and the Hollywood stars who enjoyed his Polynesian lifestyle.

CherryBlossom
Punch

The Beachcomber describes this exotic drink as
"the haunting flavors of the Orient, and reminiscent of Cherry
Blossom Time on the high slopes of Mt. Fujiyama."

1/2 ounce lime juice
1/4 ounce grenadine
1/4 ounce Hawaiian Punch
1/4 ounce Fassionola
1-1/2 ounces Puerto Rican light rum*
2 dashes each Angostura bitters - foam

Blend in blender.   * Recommended rum substitution:
                        1-1/2 ounces Ron Rico light rum

Presentation is everything

At this rule-of-thumb, Donn was one of the best. The beautiful orna-
mental presentation, hand-held fans he designed, were in full color fea-
turing his Chinese riverboat, The Hong Kong Lady, passing a wallah wallah in the middle of the harbor and announcing various daily events on
board. The back of the fan featured full-color renderings of nine of the
Beachcomber's most famous original tropical rum concoctions, including the Zombie, the Mai Tai, Navy Grog, Don's Pearl, Beachcomber's Gold,
Mystery Daiquiri, Hong Kong Lady Rum Julep, the Pearl Diver and Cherry
Blossom Punch. Each drink was flanked by a written description carefully crafted to enhance the expectations. These fans were giveaways
placed on the dining tables and bars throughout.

Mystery
Gardenia

1/2 ounce lime juice
3/4 ounce honey cream mix
1-1/2 ounces light rum
1 dash Angostura bitters

Blend in blender.

Strange As It Seems

A "Strange As It Seems" article on March 17, 1938 in the Los Angeles Daily News featured a rendering of Don the Beachcomber with the caption, "'Don the Beachcomber' —Hollywood, Cal., café man, wears a fresh lei of gardenias or other expensive flowers every day, flown from Hawai'i by Clipper planes. In 4 years he has spent $7,800 for flowers. ."

The Beachcomber would sell flower leis and other Polynesian items from an alcove just off the hallway entrance of the new Don the Beachcomber restaurant in Hollywood. This idea was a forerunner of souvenir shops in connection with some of the more famous and popular restaurants of today. At midnight every night he would present the prettiest girl with a gardenia lei.

Cobra's Fang

1/2 ounce lime juice
1/2 ounce Falernum
1/2 ounce orange juice
1/4 ounce Fassionola
1/2 ounce Jamaica dark rum*
1/2 ounce Lemon Hart Demerara 151
1 dash each Angostura bitters, selected
        herbs, grenadine

Blend all ingredients with crushed ice. Use a tall
glass and garnish with fresh mint and a lime wheel.

Recommended rum substitution:
1/2 ounce Myers's Original dark rum

Secret Recipes

In order to preserve the secrets of his drink recipes, the Beachcomber went to extreme lengths. From the beginning he realized rivals would try to raid his establishment of employees in an effort to copy his formulae. First, he removed the labels from all bottles and used a method of codes so that employees could not memorize the various ingredients and proportions of his famous concoctions. Numbers and letters were placed on the bottles. Recipes were written in code and the bartenders followed a pattern of coded symbols indicating the ingredients, which only the Beachcomber himself was allowed to mix.

COLONEL Beach's
Plantation Punch

The Beachcomber Goes To War

In February 1942 the Beachcomber received a letter from Washington informing him that he was being commissioned in the U.S. Army Air Corps. He was assigned to Casablanca. On the way over, the Beachcomber's convoy was attacked by four German U-boats, and in the torpedo blast he cracked three ribs and dislocated his right shoulder. After recovery in a French hospital, he was issued a C-47, a crew, seven hundred dollars in gold and his own Colt 45. He was ordered to set up rest camps for combat-weary airmen in Capri, Nice, Cannes, Venice, the Lido and Sorento.

"The gold," Major Doolittle told him, "is just in case you get captured. It may serve to extricate you."

The Beachcomber was awarded the Bronze Star for his efforts in France and Italy, and was promoted to Lieutenant Colonel before his honorable discharge in 1946. During his tour of duty he was the Commanding Officer of nine hotels and twelve restaurants on the Isle of Capri, ten hotels and pensions in Venice and on the Isle of Lido, and all of the major hotels used by the U.S. Air Force on the French Riviera. He also warmed the hearts and stomachs of many war-weary soldiers with his famous Beachcomber martinis and rum punches.

2 ounces Jamaica Planters Punch rum*
1 ounce Puerto Rican dark rum*
1/2 ounce Barbados rum*
2 ounces ginger beer
3/4 ounce fresh lime juice
2 dashes Angostura
2 dashes Pernod
2 dashes Falernum
1 ounce Curacao

Shake with ice. Pour into a tall Zombie glass with three (3) or four (4) cubes of ice. Decorate with a straw, stick of orange and pineapple and garden mint.

Recommended rum substitutions:

2 ounces Appleton Estate rum
1 ounce Bacardi gold rum
1/2 ounce R.L. Seale's Old Brigand Black Label rum

Cuban
Daiquiri

Perfection achieved through a mixture of fine island rum and Singapore limes.

3/4 ounce fresh lime juice
1 ounce Daiquiri mixture
1-1/2 ounces Bacardi light rum

Pour above ingredients into a blender. Twist 1/2 lime round and drip into blender. Add six (6) ounces cracked ice. Shake for 15 seconds. Strain into frozen mold, champagne bowl glass.

Rum Collectors

Don the Beachcomber and his escape to Polynesia influenced many individuals. Not only did they come to visit his restaurants to indulge in items to please the palate, some of them became collectors of rum and Polynesian memorabilia from the Beachcomber's and other copycat establishments all across the country. Jack Thorpe, a very successful businessman from Grosse Pointe Woods, Michigan, became one of the most serious collectors of rum from all over the world. Jack would travel from one restaurant to another and knew most of the Beachcomber's employees by first name. The Beachcomber befriended Jack several years before his death, and always looked upon Jack with great fondness. As of this writing, Jack is eighty-four years old, and to this day he has never opened one of his most prized possessions, a bottle of 1907, thirty-year-old Myers (V.V.O.) Rum labeled as Fine Jamaican Rum, Bottled in Jamaica. Jack was presented this as a gift from a glass showcase by the Myers attorney, G.A. Dunkley, who was the Director of Myers's Rum in Nassau, Bahama. Jack was on one of his trips in search of rare rums.

TAHITIAN
Rum Punch

3/4 ounce fresh lime
3/4 ounce fresh lime juice
1/2 ounce fresh passion fruit juice
1/2 ounce Falernum
1/2 ounce Honey Cream Mix
3/4 ounce Jamaica light rum*
3/4 ounce Bacardi rum*
1 dash Angostura bitters

Pour above ingredients into blender and add six (6) ounces cracked ice. Shake for 15 seconds and strain into special frozen molds. Serve with straws.

Note: The special ice that is molded inside the glass must be hard frozen to retain its shape during the drinking.

Recommended rum substitution:

1-1/2 ounces total of Bacardi light rum

Coconut Rum

Fresh coconut milk blended with old island rum
and served in a green spoon coconut.

3/4 ounce lime juice
1-1/2 ounces coconut milk
2 ounces Puerto Rican rum*
1 ounce Honey Cream Mix

Cut top from coconut. Pour above
ingredients into a blender and add
six (6) ounces cracked ice. Shake
for 15 seconds. Strain into opened
coconut and serve with a straw.

Recommended rum substitution:
2 ounces Bacardi light rum

Don's PEARL

White rum, tropical fruit syrup and juice of Mexican limes.
Every fifth drink mixed contains a lovely, genuine pearl.

1/2 ounce lime juice
1/2 ounce fresh passion fruit juice
1 ounce fresh guava juice
1/4 ounce Honey Cream Mix
1/4 ounce club soda
2 ounces Puerto Rican light rum*

Pour above ingredients into a
blender and shake for 1/2 minute.
Strain into a special glass.

For added excitement, add one real
pearl into every fifth creation.

Recommended rum substitution:
2 ounces Bacardi light rum

Paradise

Don the Beachcomber, host to over 23 million dinner guests at his
Don the Beachcomber restaurants, often said: "If you can't get to paradise, I'll bring it to you."

MAI Tai
THE ORIGINAL

This robust-size rum drink is to be enjoyed well after the Kona Coffee Grog and throughout the evening. With full-flavored Jamaica rum, Don the Beachcomber guarantees that this hearty rum punch will provide comfort, warm your blood, and restore your strength.

Into a mixer pour:
1-1/2 ounces Myers's Plantation rum*
1 ounce Cuban rum
3/4 ounce fresh lime juice
1 ounce fresh grapefruit juice
1/4 ounce Falernum
1/2 ounce Cointreau
2 dashes Angostura bitters
1 dash Pernod
Shell of squeezed lime
1 cup of cracked ice (size of a dime)

Shake for 1 minute on medium speed. Serve in a double old-fashioned glass. Garnish with four sprigs of mint. Add a spear of pineapple. Sip slowly through mint sprigs until desired effect results.

* Recommended rum substitutions:
1-1/2 ounces Appleton Estate
1 ounce British Navy-style rum, such as Pusser's or Lamb's

Missionary's Downfall

A refreshing combination of Mazatlan limes, fresh pineapple, and rum, touched with the fragrance of fresh English mint. An exciting new experience, the Missionary's Downfall is to be served after dinner as a refreshing dessert and to clear the palate.

1/2 ounce lime juice
1/2 ounce honey
1/2 ounce peach liqueur
1 ounce Puerto Rican light rum*
2 ounces fresh ripe pineapple
5 leaves fresh mint
6 ounces cracked ice

Pour all ingredients into a blender, add four (4) ounces cracked ice. Blend at high speed for about 1 minute or until mixture is like snow ice. Serve in a six (6) or seven (7) ounce bowl glass. Decorate with a small sprig of mint.

* Recommended rum substitution:
1 ounce Bacardi light rum

MARAMA
RUM Punch

1 ounce Jamaica rum*
1 ounce Triple Sec
4 ounces 7-Up
1 ounce lime juice
3 dashes Angostura bitters
3 dashes orgeat syrup

Pour above ingredients into a blender and shake with ice. Drop fresh lime with hull into a large glass and pour in shaken ingredients. Add sprigs of mint.

Recommended rum substitution:
1 ounce Myers's platinum rum

Freshly squeezed pineapple juice, blended with Puerto Rican rums and lime juice, served in a hollowed-out pineapple.

3/4 ounce lime juice
1/2 ounce Honey Cream Mix
1/2 ounce Fassionola
1 ounce passion fruit juice
3 ounces fresh pineapple juice
1 ounce Negrita rum*
1 ounce Puerto Rican dark rum*
2 dashes Angostura bitters
2 dashes Falernum

Pour above ingredients into a blender and add six (6) ounces cracked ice. Turn speed to high and blend for 1/2 minute. Pour into a hollowed-out pineapple and replace the top. Serve with a straw.

Note: Use a special pineapple cutter to hollow out pineapple. Cut a small V on the lip of the pineapple top for a straw to fit.

* Recommended rum substitutions:
1 ounce Ron Rico dark rum
1 ounce Bacardi gold rum

Colonel Beach's
Plantation Ambrosia

1 bottle St. James rum*
1/2 cup golden raisins
1/2 cup prunes
4 vanilla beans
1/2 cup cherries cocktail
6 strips orange peel (zest)
3/4 cup strong instant coffee
Champagne

Recommended rum substitution:

St. James Spirits Royale
Hawaiian Pineapple Rum

Pour rum into a large bottle. Soak raisins, prunes, cherries and vanilla beans in hot water. Open the vanilla beans. Add all ingredients to rum and let stand well-capped for two months.

After two months open and strain through a cheesecloth into the original St. James bottle. Add to bottle six (6) very thin orange peels—remove after two days. Make 3/4 cup strong instant coffee.

Boil three vanilla beans for 3 minutes, cool, slit open and use knife to scrape out all the little black flavor buds. Add to coffee mixture. Combine coffee mixture to rum elixir and shake.

To Serve: Fill half of a large tulip champagne glass with rum elixir. Add good, very cold champagne. Gently stir. Close eyes and sip slowly. Continue until the desired condition is apparent.

DON'S
MARTINI

I bottle Tanqueray gin or Stolichnaya vodka
I capful vermouth
Essence (zest) of lemon or lime (slice
    with a peeler to avoid any pith)

Pour a capful of vodka or gin from the top of the bottle. Replace it with the vermouth. Add the essence of lime or lemon. Screw the top of the bottle back on and place in the freezer overnight.

Serving: Take an empty and cleaned 1/2-gallon milk carton and fill it with cold water and immerse the bottle in the water. Place in the freezer for two days. Remove from the freezer and cut the milk carton away from the ice surrounding the bottle. Put the bottle covered in ice back in the freezer for 30 days. When ready, the martini will be like syrup, but exquisite.

Pineapple
Surprise

1-1/4 ounces Puerto Rican Gold
   Label rum*
1/2 ounce Lemon Hart (151 proof)
1/4 ounce Southern Comfort
1/4 ounce Triple Sec
2 ounces fresh pineapple juice
1 teaspoon sugar
3 chunks fresh pineapple
1/2 ounce fresh lime juice

Pour above ingredients in a blender
with 1 cup shaved ice. Blend to a
creamy texture and pour into a
scooped-out fresh pineapple and
serve with straws.

Recommended rum substitution:
1-1/4 ounces Appleton Special rum

Q.B. COOLER

1/2 ounce lime juice
1/2 ounce orange juice
1/4 ounce Fassionola
1/4 ounce honey
1/2 ounce club soda
1/4 ounce Falernum
1/4 ounce Lemon Hart Demerara 151
1 ounce Jamaica dark rum*
1-1/2 ounces Puerto Rican dark rum*
1 dash each Angostura bitters, Pernod, grenadine

Blend in blender.

Recommended rum substitutions:
1 ounce Myers's Original dark rum
1-1/2 ounces Bacardi gold rum

A Chance of Rain

To increase business late at night, the Beachcomber would often-times go outside and turn on a garden hose which he had affixed above his bar's corrugated metal roof. This created the illusion of rain and just enough of a reason for patrons to remain for another round or two of drinks.

ORIGINAL RUM DRINKS

49

TEST Pilot

3/4 ounce lime juice
3/4 ounce grape juice
3/4 ounce honey
3/4 ounce Ron Rico dark rum
3/4 ounce Jamaica rum*
1 ounce Lemon Hart
    Demerara 151
2 dashes each Angostura
    bitters, grenadine

Blend in blender with
six ounces cracked ice.
Serve in a double
old-fashioned glass.

** Recommended rum substitution:
3/4 ounce Myers's Original dark rum.*

B-26 Beachcomber

In his honor, Lieutenant Ed Holliday and his crew had painted the
nose of their B-26 Marauder with a replica of the Don The Beachcomber
driftwood sign which had become his trademark. Along with the Pacific
Ocean and a setting sun, the Beachcomber was painted sitting on the
beach underneath a gently swaying palm tree. The plane and crew flew
many successful missions over enemy territory. After one mission they
returned with a damaged engine and one hundred forty-six holes in the
plane's fuselage, but landed safely with no injuries to any of the crew.

WESTIndian
Plantation Potion

1 bottle Myers's Original dark rum
1/2 cup golden raisins
1/2 cup prunes
4 vanilla beans
1/2 cup bottled cherries
Orange peel
Instant coffee
Champagne

Pour rum into a large bottle. Soak raisins, prunes, cherries and vanilla beans in hot water for two hours. Open the vanilla beans. Add all to rum and let stand well-capped for two months.

Open and strain through a cheesecloth into original rum bottle.

Add six (6) very thin strips of orange peel—remove after two days. Make 3/4 cup of strong instant coffee. Boil three vanilla beans for 3 minutes. Cool, slit open, use knife to scrape out all little black flavor buds. Add to coffee mixture. Add coffee mixture to rum elixir and shake.

Fill half of a large champagne glass with rum mixture. Add good, very cold champagne to top. Gently stir. Close eyes and sip slowly. Continue until desired condition is apparent.

SHARK'S
Tooth

3/4 ounce lime juice
3/4 ounce Daiquiri mixture
1-1/2 ounces Special 15-year-old rum*

Shake with ice cubes. Strain into a
chilled cocktail glass.

Recommended rum substitution:
1-1/2 ounces Myers's Legend rum

David Niven

David Niven described the Beachcomber as he was in those days as
follows: "Don the Beachcomber who was a thin, good-looking, philosophi-
cal, raffish character, was just that—a genuine beachcomber." Once when
the Beachcomber was completely broke, it was David Niven who left the
anonymous one hundred dollar bill in a sealed envelope in the
Beachcomber's mailbox at the Garden of Allah.

VICIOUS
Virgin

3/4 ounce fresh lime juice
1/2 ounce Cointreau
1/4 ounce Falernum
1/2 ounce Puerto Rican dark rum*
1 ounce Virgin Island St. Croix rum*

Pour into blender. Add a handful of dime-size cracked ice. Blend for 15 seconds at high speed. Serve in a thin six (6) ounce champagne glass that has been frozen in a deep freezer.

Recommended rum substitutions:

1/2 ounce Bacardi dark rum   1 ounce Cruzan Light Dry rum

The Goddess

During his tour of duty in Italy, the Beachcomber's C-47 was shot down by Fascisti soldiers. The Beachcomber escaped alone on foot and hid out in a vine-covered hole, nursing a bullet wound in his shoulder. A few days later, cold, hungry and tired, he was sitting beside a small brook washing his wound when "one of god's lovely creatures stepped from the bushes." She stopped only a few feet from him and wasn't the least embarrassed as she removed all of her clothes and stepped into the water to bathe. "She was a vision of loveliness, the raven haired beauty," he later wrote of the girl. He could do nothing more than watch as she swam and played before she finally turned in his direction and smiled at him. His shoulder healed much more quickly in the next few days with the loving care of this Italian farmer's daughter. He ate well from a hidden cache of fine wine, breads and cheeses supplied by his little Italian goddess, and, setting off for his post, he swore he would return to her as soon as the war was over.

White Sands
Champagne Jubilee

1 teaspoon Falernum
4 ounces fine Cognac
3 ounces Triple Sec
1/2 teaspoon Angostura
bitters
Thin slices lime, orange,
kiwi fruit, strawberries.

Let lime, oranges, kiwi fruit and strawberries
steep in above alcohol for about 1 hour.

Add four (4) to six (6) quarts champagne
with ice (extremely chilled).

Add fresh mint leaves and serve.

Pearl Diver

A happy surprise for your taste buds, this is a subtle blend
of Hawaiian rums and tropical fruit syrup enhanced by the gentle
tartness of Punalu'u limes.

1/2 ounce lime juice
1/2 ounce grapefruit juice
1 ounce orange juice
1/2 ounce Puerto Rican dark rum*
1/2 ounce Jamaica dark rum*
1 ounce Old St. Croix rum*
1 dash Angostura bitters

Blend all ingredients but the dark rum with crushed ice.
Pour into a twelve (12) ounce glass, float the remaining
rum and garnish with fresh mint and a pineapple spear.

Recommended rum substitutions:
1/2 ounce Bacardi gold rum
1/2 ounce Myers's Original dark rum
1 ounce Cruzan Light Dry
(If you can get Old St. Croix Premium Light, use that)

Black Hole

1 good shot of vodka (90 proof)
1 good shot of gin (90 proof)
1 good shot of Drambuie
1 dash Anisette

Pour into a small glass over ice and serve.

Beachcomber's Punch

3/4 ounce lime juice
3/4 ounce Honey Cream Mix
3/4 ounce Dagger Punch Jamaica*
3/4 ounce Ron Rico dark rum
1 dash each grenadine, Angostura
    bitters, Pernod
3 dashes Falernum

Pour all above ingredients into a
blender. Add six (6) ounces cracked
ice. Shake for 15 seconds. Pour
contents into a glass and add cracked
ice if necessary to fill glass.
Decorate with a fresh pineapple
spear and cherry and fresh
mint and serve.

* Recommended rum substitution:
3/4 ounce Appleton Estate rum

Zombie

One of Don the Beachcomber's most popular drinks, it was originally created for a special friend and is to be enjoyed during the long afternoon hours. Because of its potency, a limit of two (2) per guest was established.

3/4 ounce lime juice
1/2 ounce grapefruit juice
1/2 ounce Falernum
1/2 ounce simple syrup
1-1/4 ounces Ramirez Royal Superior - Puerto Rico*
1 ounce Lemon Hart Demerara 151
1 ounce Palau (30 years old) - Cuba*
1 ounce Myers's Planter's Punch - Jamaica*
1 ounce Treasure Cove (32 years old) - Jamaica*
2 dashes each Angostura bitters, Pernod
1 dash Absinthe, Pernod
3 dashes grenadine
3/4 ounce Maraschino liqueur

Pour above ingredients into a blender. Add a handful of small cracked ice. Blend at medium speed. Pour into a fourteen (14) ounce glass with three (3) or four (4) cubes of ice. Decorate with a spear of fresh pineapple, orange, cherry, sprig of mint. Serve with a straw. Sip with eyes half-closed.

* Recommended rum substitutions:

1-1/4 ounces Captain Morgan Private stock
1 ounce Myers's Legend rum
1 ounce Appleton Estate rum
1 ounce 30-year-old Ron Zacapo Centenario rum

ORIGINAL RUM DRINKS

Navy Grog

3/4 ounce lime juice
3/4 ounce grapefruit juice
3/4 ounce honey
3/4 ounce Ron Rico dark rum*
3/4 ounce Jamaica Dagger Punch*
3/4 ounce Navy Rum (86 proof)*
3/4 ounce soda
2 dashes Angostura bitters
1 ounce fresh guava juice
8 ounces cracked ice

A robust rum punch dedicated to all gallant men of all the navies of the world.

Pour above ingredients into a blender and shake on high speed for 1/2 minute. Strain into a glass and add a special popsicle with straw inside. Serve in a fourteen (14) ounce glass.

Popsicles are to be pre-made and kept on their side so as to prevent the hole that is made during the forming of the mold from freezing over. The hole is to be kept open to receive the large straw.

* Recommended rum substitutions:

3/4 ounce Appleton Estate rum
3/4 ounce British Navy-style rum, such as Pusser's, Lamb's or Wood's

ORIGINAL RUM DRINKS

Coffee
Drinks

Tahitian Coffee

7 ounces hot coffee
1/4 ounce Cointreau
4 dashes cognac

Serve in a coffee cup with
vanilla bean.

Colonel's Favorite

6 ounces hot coffee
1/4 ounce gold rum
6 dashes Tia Maria coffee liqueur
I tablespoon whipped cream

Combine and serve in
a coffee cup, topped with
whipped cream.

Connoisseur's Note:
For best results, use Bacardi
Gold rum.

KONA
CoffeeGrog

A masterful blend of Kona coffee and fine rums,
with a dash of this and a dash of that, Kona Coffee Grog is
best served after dinner.

I cup Kona coffee
2 teaspoons honey cream mix
1/3 teaspoon cinnamon
1-1/2 ounces dark rum
4 strips lemon peel
4 strips orange peel sticks

Into a small pan pour hot Kona coffee.
Add honey. Slowly heat. Pour mixture
into a coffee grog glass. In a separate
heatproof pitcher combine rum(s),
cinnamon and citrus peels. Take
pitcher and coffee to the table. With
chopsticks, remove a piece of orange
peel and set afire. Plunge peel back
into pitcher, setting rum mixture
ablaze. Pick up flaming citrus peel and
cinnamon pieces and drop into the coffee grog
glass. Pour flaming rum(s) into glass and stir
with chopsticks and serve.

Connoisseur's Note:
*For best results, use 3/4 ounce of Ron Rico Dark and
3/4 ounce Lemon Hart Demerara 151 rums.*

COFFEE DRINKS

Cafe Diable

20 small sugar cubes
10 whole cloves
2 cinnamon sticks
1 cup brandy
4 cups double strength coffee
Peel of 1 orange (removed in a spiral)
Peel of 1 lemon (removed in a spiral)

In a chafing dish, over an open flame, combine orange peel and lemon peel with sugar cubes, cloves and cinnamon sticks. Pour over brandy and ignite carefully. While brandy is burning, pour in hot coffee. Ladle into demitasse cups.
Serves 6 generously.

African Safari

7 ounces hot coffee
1 tablespoon honey
1/2 ounce dark rum
1 twist lemon peel
Dust of nutmeg

Combine and serve in a coffee cup.

Connoisseur's Note:
For best results, use Myers's Original dark rum.

Cafe à la
Queen of Tonga

Queen Halaevalua Mata'aho, descendant to the throne
of Tonga after five hundred years of royalty, was the honored guest
for the two-day opening celebration festivities of
the Waiākea Village Resort in Hilo, along with her daughter
Princess Piloevu Tuku'aho. In the Queen's honor Don
the Beachcomber concocted the following.

1/2 cup whipping cream
1/4 teaspoon instant coffee
1/2 teaspoon cocoa
1 drop almond extract
1 light dusting of cinnamon
2 teaspoons coconut syrup
8 ounces hot Kona coffee
1/2 ounce gold rum

Blend whipping cream, instant coffee,
cocoa, almond extract and cinnamon until granules
of coffee dissolve. Whip until stiff peaks form. Into
a large cup or glass, add coconut syrup and coffee
and stir until the syrup dissolves. Add rum. Top
with a generous dollop of spiced whipped cream.
Add Tahitian vanilla bean and gently stir.

Connoisseur's Note:
For best results, use Hana Bay Premium Gold Rum.